Beautiful
Yosemite ®
National Park

Beautiful
Yosemite®
National Park

Text: Robin Will

Revisions as suggested by staff of the Yosemite Natural History Association (YNHA)

Third Edition, August, 1986
Published by Beautiful America Publishing Company
9725 S.W. Commerce Circle
Wilsonville, OR 97070
Theodore E. Paul, President

Library of Congress Cataloging in Publication Data
Beautiful Yosemite National Park
1. Yosemite National Park — Pictorial Works I. Title
F68.Y6W68   979.4'47   79-15850
ISBN 0-89802-069-7
ISBN 0-89802-068-9 (paperback)

Yosemite Falls

Photography

Contents

Introduction

There's an old saying that you don't miss the water until the well runs dry, and another equally hoary one that comments on the human tendency not to lock the barn until the horse has already run off. We treat such old proverbs with scorn; but the reason that sayings like those live to be old is that there's truth in them, in this case the homely and humbling truth that mankind tends to be wise, appreciative and prudent mostly after the fact. That is as true about the ecology as it is about anything else.

The last quarter of the 20th century, I'm sure, feels like a time of dry wells and vanished horses to many Americans. We're suddenly appreciating things we didn't know we had until they were gone, or nearly so. And we can take cold comfort from one of the yet-to-be-old sayings of the last few years, which came to us from a comic strip: ''We have met the enemy, and he is us.''

Like a great many other people, I comfort myself with statements that might be evasions; but like most other people, I'm not sure. Nobody as yet can show us the whole picture; things are likely to be neither as good nor as bad as opposing forces claim; and there is a large body of evidence to suggest that birds, trees, animals and men want to live, and somehow find ways to keep on doing so. In the atmosphere of ecological gloom that we've gotten ourselves into, it is also a comfort to see those occasions when all the old sayings have not held true. Yosemite is certainly one of those.

Yosemite was set aside as public land in 1864. It was the first time Congress had ever acted to preserve scenery, and it was the forerunner of the National Parks that we know today. Given the trends of the time, it seems something of a miracle that the plans for this very first national park reached fruition. There was no shortage of open, wild country in 1864, no lack of elbow room. The age of exploitation had barely gotten underway, and the young United States had resources to burn. The resulting smoke, in the handful of cities that could be considered oppressive, was regarded with pride, as a sign of progress. It is difficult, in reconstructing the fabric of those times, to find the thread of conservationism that led to the establishment of national parks, and

(Preceding pages) El Capitan, Bridalveil Fall, Merced River

10

eventually to the ecological awareness of our own time. Nonetheless, the miracle happened, and we have Yosemite National Park to show for it.

Yosemite—the land—is a monument to the things Mother Nature can accomplish when she's in a show-off mood. It is scenery raised to the highest order of magnitude. Yosemite—the park—is also a monument, to people who worked to preserve it even when they didn't have to. It's an example of something that was preserved before it was lost, valued before it was destroyed. It stands as a reminder that such a thing is possible.

We're offering this book to underscore the possibility that the old saws aren't irrevocably true. People will, of course, take care of Yosemite because they have to. It is tradition, and it is also the law. But we hope in addition that folks will look at the pictures, read the text, and feel inspired to take a little extra care of everything. Of course, no book can speak for Yosemite as well as Yosemite speaks for itself, but we hope this volume will serve either as a glowing introduction, or a fond reminder, of one of the truly bright spots in the world.

R.W.

Merced River, El Capitan

12

Merced River, Half Dome

13

On Wildness

One measure of a culture is what it talks about—what its language has words to express. And it is curious that our language doesn't have the words to deal comfortably with a place like Yosemite and the effect it has on people. It is, to be sure, an area of awesome natural beauty, and it contains some true wilderness. But wilderness is a term like ''solitude;'' it exists only when nobody's looking. When a group of people show up to enjoy it, the condition of solitude disappears; and wilderness likewise is diminished by degrees when ''tame'' human beings penetrate it. So, properly speaking, a great deal of Yosemite cannot be called wilderness.

However, careful management, especially in the Yosemite Valley where the pressures are great, has preserved the essence of wildness without the limits of wilderness—and by ''wildness'' can be meant broadly all those things in the world that owe nothing to mankind. Animals, trees, oceans and mountains are all wild by that measure, for none of them particularly need us. Wildness can be affected by man without altering its essence: an eagle is undeniably magnificent, even in captivity, though I don't want this to be construed as an argument for locking up eagles. A great, storm-pounded beach is not necessarily destroyed when man gains access to it; and the great Yosemite Valley is splendid even with campgrounds tucked in among the trees.

The experience of wildness, wherever he may find it, has a profound effect on man—really a series of effects. First, it makes him quiet down. Think of the enormous human silence you experience at the brink of the Grand Canyon, or on a lonely ocean point with storm-driven waves leaping sky-high off the rocks, or on the top of a mountain where men don't usually go. In places like that, folks don't have a lot to say. Words fail, silence falls, a bit awkward because it's so unaccustomed.

Eventually in the wild something replaces the silence, something every bit as rare as the silence was, and that is good talk. Good talk is hard to define but easy to recognize: it's like singing in tune, where the pleasure is not in the message as much as the harmony. Words, when they come, carry a cargo of warmth and contentment.

If that mood is allowed to run its course, another one slips in beneath it: talk starts to flag and folks start itching to *do* something. They start to play: a Frisbee comes out of a backpack; somebody rolls up his pants and gets into the river; a side canyon suddenly just begs to be explored or a cliff climbed, and suddenly everybody is grinning as if they have just been set free.

Some people require bigger doses of wildness than others. Some admire the view, skip rocks in the creek or stroll under the trees. Others climb mountains, or spend weeks on the trails. But few are altogether immune. That's why we need wildness; and though we often find it at cross purposes with our lifestyle, it cannot be the wildness that's at fault. We must recognize that in some deep and almost spiritual way, we need trees, pretty stretches of riverbank, and eagles much more than they need us. They, after all, are already free.

John Muir, who spent half a lifetime entertaining himself in Yosemite, obviously knew the feeling. "And surely," he wrote in *Boyhood and Youth,* "all God's people, however serious and savage, great or small, like to play. Whales and elephants, dancing, humming gnats, and invisibly small mischievous microbes—all are warm with divine radium and must have lots of fun in them." Muir knew there was play in wildness, and also that there was wildness in play. He wrote time and again that he felt his freest and best in the wilderness of the High Sierra.

John Muir is far from the only human being who ever noticed that an encounter with nature made him feel good. Anybody who has ever spent an afternoon jumping waves in the ocean or skipping rocks across a creek has felt it, and perhaps wondered later just why such simple activity had seemed so absorbing at the time: why did it feel like being set free?

The answer is enigmatic: we get set free by being put in our place. That may seem curious, even contradictory. We are told and told that men should be free; and that, with our opposed thumbs and curious brains, we're capable of almost anything. That seems to be all too true. But man's creations cause him a lot of worry: there's a lot of effort in putting up a dam, an airplane, or a government, and more yet in keeping them up. In the long run they're no more perfect than we are, and we know it; and when they come down, it's usually somebody's fault, and we all would rather it were not ours. We become anxious slaves to our creations.

Given the anxiety that underlies most of our waking activity and a lot of our dreams, it is a great relief to be handed occasionally a moment in which we are powerless . . . and that's what wildness does. The tide comes in, and we can't do anything about it except get out of the way; the canyon is there, and we don't have to

Tenaya Lake

Mt. Dana

Yosemite Falls from Falls Trail

18

Sawtooth Ridge from Twin Lakes
(Overleaf) Mt. Dana

19

Yosemite Falls

Lower Yosemite Falls

23

Yosemite Falls

Deer in Yosemite Valley

Pywiack Dome

Half Dome

Half Dome, late evening

Dogwood in Yosemite Valley

30

Yosemite Falls, Yosemite Point

31

Tenaya River

Mt. Gibbs near Touloume Meadows

33

form a committee to decide it; the face of the mountain is steep and sheer, and if we approach it, we do so on the mountain's terms. Of course, we can do things *to* wildness, given time to rally our forces: bulldozers, chainsaws and dynamite may have their way in time. But that's usually not man's first response to wildness— the personal response. At the first hint that there are parts of creation that do not require man's presence to do their work—the mere suggestion that man occupies a tiny corner in creation and not the pinnacle—man tends to relax. It gets him off the hook, and sets him free. And once he's free of the demands we consider ''real life,'' he is free to meet fellow man and environment in some fairly simple and direct ways . . . and to play.

History and Such

Even in the annals of the world's wild and beautiful places, Yosemite has been considered special for as long as it has been known to human beings. It is as if you could focus life through a magnifying glass like you focus sunbeams to make a fire, creating in one small area a zone of life much more highly concentrated than anywhere else. It's a strange concept to have in our world, where something is either alive or it isn't, and we believe we know the difference, but a lot of otherwise sane visitors to the valley have made similar reflections upon what they saw.

"Yonder stands the South Dome," wrote John Muir in *My First Summer in the Sierra,* "its crown high above our camp, though its base is four thousand feet below us; a most noble rock, it seems full of thought, clothed with living light, no sense of dead stone about it, all spiritualized, neither heavy looking nor light, steadfast in serene strength like a god."

The original inhabitants of the valley, the Ahwahneechees, in fact did believe that the rocks and hills were alive. The great stone eminences grew up with the tribe, getting bigger year by year. A collection of legends from the Indians, who came to be known as the Uzumati (Yosemite), possibly from their word for "grizzly bear," was published shortly after the turn of the century by Galen Clark, discoverer of the Mariposa Grove and one of the first Guardians of the Yosemite Valley. The stories speak of the origins of the big monoliths—sometimes, in fact, citing more than one origin, and more than one name, for each stone. But taken together, they indicate that the Indians, too, saw the Yosemite Valley as a living thing.

Along with the general feeling that things are more alive at Yosemite than elsewhere—perhaps because of it—an overall good humor pervades. The inimitable Muir said it best: "God himself always seems to be doing his best here, working like a man in a glow of enthusiasm." It is even harder to explain good-natured trees, rivers and mountains than to accept the notion of a place infused with a greater-than-normal amount of life. Or maybe it isn't, especially if you're standing in one of the meadows along the sparkling Merced as evening falls, watching the day's last light on the monoliths above the valley and the contentment on the faces of passers-by. Even the names of the landmarks carry positive connotations: there isn't a "Devil's

anything'' in the valley, and hasn't been since the very early days when white men decided to hang Lost Arrow with the monicker ''Devil's Thumb.'' It didn't take, and the old Indian name was restored.

There may be rational or aesthetic explanations for the effect of good-natured liveliness that the Yosemite Valley projects. One thing that suggests itself is the nature of the scenery there: clear river, grassy meadows, handsome trees, stony cliffs—all commonplace phenomena, familiar things that are here raised to the superlative. There are no boiling mudpots, steaming geysers, stony, tortured landscapes or weirdly-eroded rock forms, nothing spooky or scary. Instead there is a collection of superlatives that, if taken one by one, would suffice to endow dozens of parks. All over the United States, single waterfalls much smaller than Yosemite Falls—or any of the others—are enshrined in state and local reserves; elsewhere in the country are rivers, grasslands and forests set aside for public enjoyment, or single stony peaks swarmed over by climbers and onlookers. But it took Yosemite to get it all together.

John Muir thought the overall effect had to do with the delicate but massive proportions of the valley. ''The magnitudes of rocks and trees and streams are so delicately harmonized they are mostly hidden,'' he wrote in *My First Summer in the Sierra.* ''Sheer precipices three thousand feet high are fringed with tall trees growing close like grass on the brow of a lowland hill, and extending along the feet of these precipices a ribbon of meadow a mile wide and seven or eight long, that seems like a strip a farmer might mow in less than a day. Waterfalls five hundred to one or two thousand feet high are so subordinated to the mighty cliffs over which they pour that they seem like wisps of smoke, gentle as floating clouds, though their voices fill the valley and make the rocks tremble . . . any attempt to appreciate any one feature is beaten down by the overwhelming influence of all the others.'' Muir's comment seems to be borne out by first-time visitors to the valley, who find it much bigger and grander than they had expected from the photographs.

But in the long run, an analysis of the features and proportions of the Yosemite Valley bears very little fruit. It's possible to take a clock apart and comment that it consists of wheels, springs and gears of various sizes without adding much to the general understanding of clocks. To say that Yosemite consists of mountains, waterfalls, some meadows and a river is futile: we couldn't make another one even if we did have the recipe. In such cases, the older stories are the best: they're shorter, answer just as many questions, and show a lot more imagination than modern atempts. Combining the best of Muir and the Indians, we can claim that the particular vibrancy of the Yosemite Valley happens because the mountains grew up there from little boulders, and that God was happy with the results.

Of the Indians who first inhabited the valley relatively little is known. Their own tribal legends describe the Awahneechees as a formerly great people who fell upon bad times when they were deserted by a favored leader. Their story tells not only of the tribe's fall from grace, but also explains the formation of a pair of the valley's landmarks: El Capitan and Half Dome; and the origin of one of the Awahneechee's principal crafts, the art of basketmaking.

In the days when the mountains were still growing around the valley Awahnee, Chief Choo-too-se-ka built a palace lodge on El Capitan, and had his mighty chair of state a short distance from his lodge, where on festive occasions he could look over the valley and speak to the assembled multitudes. Fair Tis-sa-ack came from the south, asking permission to rest in the valley a while before returning to her home, and during her stay, she taught the tribe to make baskets.

The great chief fell in love with Tis-sa-ack, and built her a lodge on Half Dome (which was not just a half-dome then), and visited her there often, asking for her hand in marriage. But Tis-sa-ack steadfastly refused, and one night she slipped away in the darkness. The lovesick chief forgot his people and went to search for her, and never returned.

That was the beginning of a series of calamities that very nearly destroyed the Awahneechees. An earthquake split Half Dome, leaving it in the shape it's in today, and the silhouette of the monolith, reminiscent of the straight-banged hairstyle of the Awahneechee women, caused the name Tissa-ack to be accorded it. Then there was a drought, a flood, volcanic action and a "black sickness" that eventually made the weakened tribe flee the valley, leaving it uninhabited for many years.

By the time the white settlers came to the Sierra, Miwok people had established permanent villages in Yosemite Valley along the Merced River. They called Yosemite Valley, "Ah-wah-nee", meaning "place of the gaping mouth". With the discovery of gold in 1848, came the sudden influx of thousands of people into the Mariposa region. Resentment grew between the Indians and the gold seekers as the Indians who were displaced raided for food and whose raids were met with violence. A group of state volunteers known as the Mariposa Battalion and commanded by Major James D. Savage was dispatched to subdue the Indians. Yosemite Valley was discovered by these men in March, 1851. Captain John Boling, whose company was part of the Mariposa Battalion, led a second expedition against the Yosemites in May, 1851. One of Chief Tenaya's beloved sons was killed by the soldiers and Captain Boling continued to pursue the Indians into the high country. His soldiers surprised the band in their camp at Tenaya Lake and, after the Indians surrendered, began with them the

(Following page) Yosemite Falls

journey to the Fresno reservation. Tenaya promised he would provoke no further trouble and was soon permitted to return to Yosemite Valley, where he was joined by other members of his band who managed to leave the reservation. After his death in 1853, the Yosemite Indians dispersed as the Ahwahneechees had done years before, some staying on the east side of the Sierra with the Mono Lake Paiutes, some living with the Miwok bands along the Tuolumne River, and some returning to Yosemite valley again.

Almost from the time Yosemite was discovered by Americans, there was talk about the need to preserve it, but there was some difficulty in figuring out exactly how. Travelers were penetrating the valley in some numbers by 1860, an arduous trip on horseback through summer's heat and dust, and California began to realize that in Yosemite it had a rare treasure. In 1864 President Lincoln signed a bill to grant a large tract of land containing the valley and the Mariposa Grove of Big Trees to the State of California. It was the first time Congress had ever acted to preserve scenery. In 1890 the Park was ''locked up'' by a large area designated as forest preserve, surrounding the state-controlled Yosemite Valley, and it became known as Yosemite National Park. In 1893, the Sierra Forest Reserve was created, ringing the national park; and in 1906, after some difficulty coordinating the park's dual administrations, the State of California ceded the Yosemite Valley back to the Federal government.

The reason for this continuing change in the status of Yosemite in the early days was concern that commercial exploitation would ruin ''the Yosemite,'' and effective pressure from conservationist forces to do something about it. The vanguard of conservationist forces was the Sierra Club, an organization which has become almost synonymous with Yosemite in the years since its founding. John Muir had arrived in California in 1868 and had proceeded almost straight to Yosemite, spending a large portion of the rest of his life in the valley. But it was not until 1892 that a group of wilderness-loving individuals gathered to form the Sierra Club, a group to concern itself with advocacy for wilderness. John Muir was the club's first president.

There were plenty of problems for the group to work on. Mining and lumber interests would have preferred that there be no park at all, and there were objections to preserving the headwaters of the Merced and the Tuolumne Rivers. Sheep and cattlemen wanted the lands for grazing. A few individuals had staked private claims in the valley, and out of stubbornness or an urge to capitalize on future benefits, they didn't want to leave. While the valley was under control of the State of California, many usage decisions made by the commissioners of the park were of greater benefit to the commissioners than to the park.

In spite of all that, some of Yosemite's greatest danger came from the people who loved it. Hotels in the valley were of necessity accompanied by livery stables and dairy barns, which in turn were accompanied by the very necessary hayfields and cow pastures. Early photographs show the valley cleared and fenced with barbed wire, the native meadows plowed and planted to hay and groves of oak trees logged. Recession of the valley to the Federal government in 1906 opened the way to more impartial and evenhanded management, and continued advocacy from the Sierra Club helped formulate the intelligent policies of the National Park Service as it exists today.

Most of those problems are far in the past, and if it was necessary to name the single bugaboo of Yosemite's present, it would have to be overcrowding. Hordes of visitors place a severe burden on land that is fundamentally in its natural state, and the irony of traffic jams in the wilderness was once a daily fact of life in the Yosemite Valley. But in the last four or five years, the National Park Service has been successful in separating Americans, at least temporarily, from their automobiles, and the crush has eased a little. A system of one-way traffic in the valley, along with free shuttle service, keeps auto traffic minimal when more than 40,000 people crowd the park on a summer weekend. Park officials are studying other ways to coax tourists out of their cars for the duration of their stay at Yosemite.

All this talk about the Yosemite Valley, however, neglects an important fact: the valley is less than a tenth of the total National Park. The rest is roadless wilderness with all the glory of the High Sierras. This area sometimes bears the burden of overuse as Americans' interest in outdoor recreation increases, but it is recognized that the further you get from the valley, the fewer people you meet. It's still possible for the devoted backpacker to find himself alone in the silence of the mountains.

The long suit of Yosemite is its variety. It's possible to stay in a luxurious hotel, park a motor home, or camp in a tent. Activities range from none in the back-country through a variety of walks, tours and discussions by the dedicated National Park personnel. In the evening, square dances, films and astronomy walks may occupy the visitor in the valley, while in the back-country visitors may feel as if they have the stars to themselves. There are ways for everyone to enjoy Yosemite.

Sentinel Rock

El Capitan, Merced River

45

The Valley

Mark Twain once conjectured that when God made the North American continent, He must have worked from east to west. Working against a stiff deadline, He was compelled to build with whatever He had on hand. That, Twain asserted, explained the deserts of the Southwest: God just couldn't wait for the next shipment of materials, so He built what he could out of rock and sagebrush.

The Yosemite Valley may be a piece of evidence in support of that peculiar theory, or a continuation of it. When the Almighty finally got the shipment of materials He needed to complete the continent, He found he had several waterfalls and some granite monoliths that had to be used before He built the coastline. And since He was in a hurry, He put them all in one seven-mile valley and called it Yosemite. That is one slightly unconventional explanation for the fact that there are seven major waterfalls and five granite peaks within this small area in the Sierra Nevada.

There are other explanations. The Sierra Nevada is a range of block mountains—in a sense, one mountain all of granite—pushed up from the earth millions of years ago. The Yosemite Valley probably began as a fissure between huge plates of granite. An ice sheet about 3,000 feet thick gouged the valley to nearly its present width and depth and then melted, turning it into a lake, dammed probably by earthquake debris, which deposited a nearly-flat layer of glacial debris on the bottom. Then the lake dwindled and disappeared, leaving the meandering Merced River, fed by springs and the waterfalls that plunge from the cliffs.

The largest of the waterfalls is Yosemite. It drops 1,430 feet uninterrupted, and then after some rugged cataracts, drops about 320 feet more. From the crest to the bottom of the valley, counting the cascades in between, the total drop of Yosemite Falls is 2,545 feet. Tremors from this downpour shake the valley floor for a half-mile around.

Bridalveil falls 620 feet, and seems to have gotten its name for the tendency of the waterfall to blow in the wind like a giant veil. When the sun gets low in the afternoon, it's possible from some vantage points in the valley to watch a rainbow climb Bridalveil's misty column. Of all the sights in the valley, wrote John Muir in *The Yosemite,* "... perhaps the first to fix our attention will be the Bridal Veil, a beautiful waterfall on our right. Its brow, where it first leaps free from the cliff, is about nine hundred feet above us; and as it sways and sings in the wind, clad in gauzy, sun-sifted spray, half-falling, half-floating, it seems infinitely gentle and fine; but the hymns it sings tell the solemn, fateful power hidden beneath its soft clothing."

Fateful power, indeed; in another place Muir writes of an afternoon spent trying to get behind Yosemite Falls, waiting for the wind to move the column of water so he could slip past to view the moon through the waterfall. He got soaked and was hammered against the rocks by the weight of the falling water, learning firsthand the power of the "gauzy, sun-sifted spray."

Few places in the Yosemite Valley are out of sight or sound of falling water. Ribbon Fall drops from the valley's rim some 1,612 feet, and the Merced River itself crashes into the valley over Vernal Fall (317 feet) and over Nevada Fall (594 feet). The latter two are the most dependable of the valley's waterworks: the mountain streams that feed the others shrink in the dry season to mere wisps, but the Merced runs in considerable volume the year around.

The waterfalls are high above the valley floor, but above the waterfalls are the monoliths, the huge granite domes, towers and pinnacles that catch morning's first sun and the last rays of sunset. The word "monolith" is made of two Greek words which mean "single stone," and Yosemite seems to provide the features for which the word was made. In *The Yosemite,* John Muir described these monuments with typical exuberance: "... no temple made with hands can compare with Yosemite. Every rock in its walls seems to glow with life. Some lean back in majestic repose; others, absolutely sheer or nearly so for thousands of feet, advance beyond their companions in thoughtful attitudes, giving welcome to storms and calms alike, seemingly aware, yet heedless, of everything going on about them. Awful in stern, immovable majesty, how softly these rocks are adorned, and how fine and reassuring the company they keep: their feet among beautiful groves and meadows, their brows in the sky...."

Legend has it that two small boys, drying out after a swim in the Merced, climbed up on a sun-warmed boulder for a nap. As they slept, the boulder grew to the stature of El Capitan. All the animals in the valley gathered to try to bring the sleeping boys down from the rock, but none could leap far enough up the sheer face of the cliff. Finally the humble measuring worm, despised by the other animals, came silently forward and started to inch his way up the cliff, eventually reaching the

Bridalveil Fall

Yosemite Valley in Winter
(Overleaf) Cathedral Peak and Touloume River

Three Brothers and Merced River

51

Touloume Meadows

Vernal Fall from Mist Trail
(Overleaf) Half Dome from Glacier Point

Sequoia Trees

Vernal Fall

58

Illilouette Fall

North Dome in autumn

60

Half Dome at Sunrise

Lambert Dome, Touloume River

Mist-Shrouded El Capitan

El Capitan

sleepers and carrying them down to safety. In memory of the event, the mighty bulk of El Capitan was named, in the Indian language, for the measuring worm.

The legend about the origin of Half Dome (Tis-sa-ack) states that the woman (Tis-sa-ack) came to the valley Ahwahnee with her husband. Thirsty from a day's travel, the couple stopped at Mirror Lake, and Tis-sa-ack, drinking first, drank until the lake was dry, leaving no water for her husband. Angry, he forgot the customs of his people and began to beat her with a stick; she ran from him, but he followed and beat her again. Finally in her anger she turned on him, reviled him, and threw her basket at him. In this attitude they were turned to stone for their wickedness. ''The upturned basket,'' relates Galen Clark, ''lies beside the husband, where the woman threw it, and the woman's face is tear-stained, with long dark lines trailing down. Half Dome is the woman Tis-sa-ack and North Dome is her husband, while beside the latter is a smaller dome which is still called Basket Dome to this day.''

Entry to the Yosemite Valley is from the west, up the Merced River from the Arch Rock entrance station, Oak Fork Road from the north, or Wawona Road from the south. Probably the folks who drive up from Wawona and the Mariposa Grove have the best initial view, although there is no such thing as a bad view here. Wawona Road ducks into a tunnel 4,233 feet long, and emerges into sunlight in the valley. Bridalveil, wispy or torrential depending on the season, cascades down a sheer cliff on the right; El Capitan stands serene and beautiful on the left; and between them, the cliffs, forests and meadows line the clear and sparkling Merced River. Beyond that, the view closes in as the valley makes a slight bend, but overall towers Half Dome, which at 8,842 feet lords it over the rest of the Yosemite monoliths.

A short drive up the valley takes you past the curve, beyond Cathedral Rocks and Three Brothers, beyond the cluster of campgrounds and Yosemite Village, to a spot where the valley forks. The top end of the valley is split by Half Dome, and the north fork is called Tenaya Canyon after the creek which flows there. At Yosemite Village, Curry Village, or the Ahwahnee Hotel, it's time to park the car and look for one of the park's shuttle buses, untrap the bicycles from the bike rack, or get ready for a walk. The ban on private auto traffic in this end of the park has had a variety of good effects: it makes the road safer for hikers and cyclists; it keeps autos out of the way of the big shuttle buses; and it gives people who would otherwise be driving a chance to look at the magnificent landscape.

There's plenty of looking to be done. To the north, Tenaya Canyon is the home of placid Mirror Lake and the head of the trail to Tuolumne Meadows. The gorge of the Merced continues to the south, and that's where you'll find Vernal and Nevada Falls. The Mist Trail offers a short loop around the two waterfalls, and hikers should be advised that there is more truth than poetry in the name. A lot of the Merced, instead of going over the falls, seems to hang in the air instead.

The person who wants to see it all together, and is prepared for a hike, can ascend to Glacier Point. At 7,214 feet, the point stands more than 4,000 feet above the valley floor, facing Half Dome across the Merced River. At the foot of Half Dome is Mirror Lake, fed by Tenaya Creek, and beyond that, Tenaya Canyon narrows, forested at the bottom but with walls of glacier-polished stone. To the other side of Half Dome, the canyon of the Merced presents its waterfalls to view.

Hikers may reach Glacier Point via the Panorama Trail, above Vernal Falls, or from downstream via the Four Mile Trail, which originates in the valley near Sentinel Creek. Motorists may drive there on Glacier Point Road, which leaves Wawona Road at Chinquapin Junction, south of the valley. The road is closed in winter.

(Overleaf) Vernal and Nevada Falls from Glacier Point

The Big Trees

Sequoiadendron giganteum, the Big Trees, are the biggest living things on earth, and among the oldest; and three groves of them are found within the borders of Yosemite National Park. Even in a place like Yosemite, where natural wonders are found closer together than elsewhere, the groves of Mariposa, Tuolumne and Merced occupy special positions of reverence. Mariposa was preserved with the original Federal grant of 1864; the others were added to the park as boundaries were changed later.

It is almost always silent in a grove of Big Trees, save for the murmur of branches far overhead in some unnoticed breeze. People find themselves without much to say. It is almost always dark in a grove of Big Trees as well: not much light reaches the floor through the canopy of branches overhead. One photographer in the Mariposa Grove, aside from the challenge of fitting Grizzly Giant into his viewfinder, also discovered that he had to work fast: the trunk of the tree was illuminated by sunlight for only about 15 minutes in the early afternoon, when the sun was almost directly overhead. A stand of sequoias, massive trunks reaching skyward, shedding a carpet of needles onto the bare forest floor, resembles a giant cathedral.

John Muir, who believed that all wilderness was a cathedral, commented, ''I never saw a Big Tree that died a normal death; barring accidents, they seem to be immortal, being exempt from all the diseases that afflict and kill other trees.'' Grizzly Giant, the biggest tree of the Mariposa Grove, is estimated to be 3,000 years old, an age that only the wizened Bristlecone Pine can match. But the Bristlecone, in its high and dry environment, has not the grandeur and the distinction of sheer size that accompanies the great age of the Big Trees. A Sequoia does not come of age, according to Muir, until it is big enough to be struck by lightning. Sometimes that particular honor is a long time coming, and the Sequoia alone is able to wait for it. Eventually, however, it happens—and this accounts for the heavyset appearance of the oldtimers in a grove. The really big, old ones have had their tops blown out by lightning . . . some of them several times. Grizzly Giant has a base diameter of 30 feet, a girth of more than 94 feet, and stands 200 or so feet tall. It might have gotten taller, except for lightning; but it will probably get taller yet—it's still growing.

For some reason difficult to fathom, tunnel trees have long been popular with American tourists. Rare is the person who has not seen a snapshot or picture postcard of an automobile driving through a growing tree. One might think this practice is one of the automobile age's sillier preoccupations, but the popularity of the tunnel tree in fact predates the automobile. The Wawona Tunnel Tree, once one of the most photographed of the Mariposa Grove's Big Trees, had its tunnel cut in 1881, 8 feet wide, 10 feet high, and 26 feet long. This particular tunnel tree fell during winter storms in 1969, but another in the same grove, the California Tree, still stands. In Tuolumne Grove, off Big Oak Flat Road, a 40-foot stump called Dead Giant maintains the tunnel tree tradition.

But the drive-through tree may yet become a thing of the past, at least in the Mariposa Grove, for the simple reason that private automobiles are no longer allowed there. Sheer numbers became too great: the auto was at once a means to get to somewhere as extraordinary as the Grove, and the reason folks couldn't enjoy it once they got there. Now motorists park outside and take a quiet, open motor tram through the Grove. It's a small tradeoff for the motorist: you can't see much of the Big Trees through a car window anyway, and somebody always had to worry about driving. On the tram, everybody gets to stare, and it is a treat just to watch the faces of the people who ride through the Mariposa Grove, leaning back to stare at the treetops far above them.

Once inside the grove, it's a good idea to take a walk. The duff on the forest floor—dried remains of thousands of years of dropped needles—absorbs sound and cushions the feet. Benches are thoughtfully provided throughout Mariposa, to make it easier to adopt the standard posture for observing these giants—leaning back and looking up. An alternate and completely appropriate way to accomplish the same thing is to lean against one Big Tree so as to steady yourself for a long look at another.

A solitary walk through a grove of Big Trees is usually all it takes to convince a person, if he's not already convinced, that John Muir was correct in referring to the groves as temples. In their quiet, the soaring vertical lines of the grey-brown tree trunks, the light filtering through breaks in the canopy far overhead, and the proportions which are so far beyond the scope of man, the groves do, indeed, resemble temples. But that might just be backwards. It is not as much that the trees look like temples; it is temples that look like these awesome trees, and the more magnificent the temple, the closer the resemblance. The original plan is here.

(Overleaf) Yosemite Valley from Tunnel parking lot

71

The Ninety-Nine
Per Cent

When they hear the word "Yosemite," most people think of the valley. That's understandable—the valley is the heart of the park, most accommodations exist there, and the natural features which win recognition throughout the world are concentrated there. But the seven-square-mile Yosemite Valley is less than one percent of Yosemite National Park; and there's plenty to see and do in the other ninety-nine as well.

To do a good job of seeing Yosemite requires a certain amount of peace of mind, knowing that there's always going to be something you miss. If a person were "taking" Yosemite like you take a course in school, getting graded on how much you do and how neatly, then it might be possible to dash through the park and see it all . . . if you call that "seeing." But Yosemite lends itself to a different sort of experience: it starts out great, and then grows on you. A visitor needs to give it time to grow. So the most important thing to remember about Yosemite is that you can always come back. Then you can settle down to enjoying where you are.

Yosemite offers wilderness in varying doses, so the visitor, like a cautious swimmer, can test by dipping in a toe before diving in. The valley offers the least in terms of wilderness because it is the place most people go to, although the forests, meadows and rivers remain in their natural state. On the other side of the park, Tuolumne Meadows is a focal point for activity of the human kind, disturbing the environment as little as possible, but still gathering humans in numbers that make them the predominant species in the area.

The Yosemite Valley and Tuolumne Meadows serve as the gateways to the more wild wilderness experience. From the valley, trails run up the Little Yosemite Valley, Yosemite Creek and Tenaya Canyon, all eventually ending on the Tuolumne River. Along some of these trails, the Yosemite Park and Curry Company runs permanent camps for those hikers who don't care to pack their own provisions and sleeping bags. The High Sierra Camps are scattered about ten miles apart, primarily in the area south of the Tuolumne River, so it's seldom more than a day's hike from one to the next.

North of the Tuolumne, it's a different story. Beyond Glen Aulin and its environs, the hiker on foot or horseback is likely to have mostly himself for company. Matterhorn Canyon is two days on horseback from the nearest paved road; and at the top of the canyon, Burro Pass leads to further trails into the silent mountains, to Pate Valley or distant Jack Main Canyon. Other hikers are few and far between, and coyotes sing the lullabies that put you to sleep at night.

The scenery through the Sierra back-country is rocky and rugged, studded with lakes and wooded meadows. The peaks are bare, sometimes scoured by the glacial action that shaped so much of this land. Plant life in the Sierra is not as much a question of climate as it is of soil, and most of the trees grow in draws and valleys below the bare granite peaks, where sufficient topsoil has managed to collect. The broad, grassy meadows which are typical of this country frequently had their origin as shallow lakes made of glacial meltwater, which gradually silted up or filled with vegetation. Other small pockets of soil support hardy alpine trees or smaller plants.

Once a person is committed to getting off the paved roads and into the back-country, the Tuolumne River is nearly unavoidable. Not that anyone would want to avoid it: it flows from east to west across Yosemite and, except where impounded in the Hetch Hetchy Reservoir, puts on quite a show for hikers who labor along its banks. Waterfalls, rapids, and steep-walled granite canyons provide ample reward for the backpackers and travelers on horseback who share the river primarily with wild animals. Probably the majority of hikers begin at Tuolumne Meadows and hike downstream as far as the Glen Aulin High Sierra Camp, one of the permanent back-country camps. Glen Aulin—a Gaelic name that means "happy glen," sits on the Tuolumne above a particularly fine cascade which is only the beginning of the Tuolumne's antics before it is stilled in the depths of the Hetch Hetchy reservoir some 15 miles away.

Beyond Glen Aulin, the trail parallels the Tuolumne, offering spectacular river scenery on one hand and several routes into the isolated northern segment of the park on the other. Along the river in quick succession are California Falls and Le Conte Falls, then the incredible Waterwheel Falls, where a granite chute tosses water into the sky. This area is known as the Grand Canyon of the Tuolumne for reasons obvious to those who have seen it; and the hiker on foot or muleback traverses the rugged Muir Gorge on a narrow trail high above the water. Many horsemen have commented about the fingerprints they left in their saddle horns over this stretch of trail, holding on with everything they had and trying not to look down to the white

Mirror Lake

Unicorn Peak and Touloume River

water below. Trails at Glen Aulin and the Pate Valley take off in a northerly direction for Matterhorn Canyon, Burro Pass, Jack Main Canyon—a rugged and infrequently visited area studded with lakes.

Eventually the trail crosses the river and heads south toward Tioga Road and civilization. The numbers of people on the trail increase in direct proportion to the distance that remains to Yosemite Valley, but most back-country hikers don't mind the return to comfortable beds, hot showers and meals that don't come out of a backpack. The cares of the rest of the world return soon enough, but for the wilderness traveler there's a difference: he can always return later.

That, in fact, is one of the greatest benefits of wilderness, and most familiar to those people who have been there. It is a good feeling simply to know that the wilderness is still there, and that it's possible to go back. The office worker can stare out his window at traffic in the street and recall an afternoon in a back-country meadow; the teacher in a noisy classroom can dream of the silence of a grove of Big Trees; the machinist can meditate on the perfect trout stream, dappled with shadows from the overhanging trees. The memory of a day or a week in the wilderness can last a long time, made all the more vivid when you know that the wilderness is still there . . . waiting.

(Following page) Higher Cathedral Spire